<the sadness of the snow>
by elena botts

TRANSCENDENT ZERO PRESS

HOUSTON, TEXAS

PUBLISHED BY TRANSCENDENT ZERO PRESS
www.transcendentzeropress.org

ISBN-13: 978-1946460936

ISBN-10: 1946460931

Printed in the United States of America

Library of Congress Control Number: 2017939050

Transcendent Zero Press
16429 El Camino Real Apt. 7
Houston, Texas 77062

Cover design by Glynn Monroe Irby
Cover photo taken by Elena Botts

FIRST EDITION
Transcendent Zero Press

<the sadness of the snow>
by elena botts

previous publishers acknowledged at elenabotts.com

dedicated to any who didn't get enough love. and to Ginger, Daisy, Fluffy, James Millard, Michelle Buck, Bob Lay, & Elizabeth Botts

Introduction

There are only so many words in the dictionary yet it is the way those words are strung together that determines a writer's style and voice. Elena Botts' verbal arrangements evoke a multitude of moods, her phrasings unraveling in ways you wouldn't expect a regular sentence or even a poem to, yet somehow it all makes evocative sense, as with:

"nobody walking through the midnight snow tasting its universe".

Throughout *the sadness of the snow* Botts explores the significance of life and the question of self-identity amid the ever unfolding Naturescape; plus she touches on what is beyond the earthly dimension:

"we are all gentle no ones treading or tossing because i remember how like a sea
it was when i craved to move fingers through the terrible quivering skiffs destined for no place."

Her poems, often sounding like thinking-out-loud monologues, address issues of the soul, and of relationships:

"and he says to me, you know you're all I got, and I said, no, there's this everlasting light,
see, just beyond the window and so infinite"

My advice to readers unfamiliar with surreal imagery, atypical grammatical structure, and stream-of-consciousness poetry is to catch what you can and let the feeling of it all carry you along. Like a Bob Dylan song where you can't always follow the logic, in every poem there's a gem of a line that you could hang out with and ponder like a photograph or a Zen koan.

At the end of this expansive book which doesn't end because you'll probably want to read it again, you may find yourself knowing exactly what Elena Botts is getting at when she writes:

"we traveled far but could find no finite spaces."

the sadness of snow reminds us that all of Nature has feelings, too, and there is a 1932 Lakota prophecy, from John Hollowhorn, which foggily mirrors the book's title:

"Some day the earth will weep, she will beg for her life, she will cry with tears of blood. You will make a choice, if you will help her or let her die, and when she dies, you too will die."

Let the lush imagery of this intricate collection of unusual poems help you to experience the beauty of earth and of all life, because

*"... everything is in
every thing, the universe is in you. all that remains is how you remember."*

- Mankh (Walter E. Harris III),
  author/editor of fifteen books, including
  Musings with the Golden Sparrow

<u>the sadness of the snow</u>
though the sky is all heavy but after the snowflakes flutter in unreality
it gets all dim and otherworldly and suddenly it's just you and your
breath and it's oddly comforting, the universe snug against your chin;
he was like a beauteous oblivion pressing up against my skin
the stars are talking only to your own small darkness. the stars are
talking only to your own small darkness.
the stars are talking only about you too. so much happened but I don't
know if you are a stranger to be in my room and I don't know

blithewood
when the trees shivering pyres of warm-like color fire

and contemplation of bay so grey centered,
reflective of the sky (her eyes)-
we, wading into the nothing.

into the there was an aftermath here once, there was a grand garden
and a story, oh yes a story and the brave blushing people in their finery
and the flowers, all dripping hyacinth, dahlia, aster in flown stars of
summer fallen into the ground and even the sky was larger somehow
but then

mansion brick might realize itself shocked whiter under the moon,
even our little radiances as we realized ourselves, impossibly standing
under

the sky infinite

just bare somethings in the dark, just forever

always expiring, well better then! the unimaginable

<u>if only the world were real,</u> you know what she'd say, i am tired today i sit in midst of a guide to birds doing silly insincerities for the men in the field those old guys all dying in a meadow hyacinth and merry haze of moth, all bitten in burrs or lighter husked wishes to be borne on a wind somewhere i wonder if spring if ever she'll show the myth of being is a funny one i think of my oblivion space when i think of you too i don't hang clothesline on the hours of your deadweight life except how are you sleeping but oh i hope the ships of dreaming are drenched deep in iridescent wells of thoughtless hells and messed up brains for us all to wade into limbo she says sorry i'm so quietly and i say but why and she says because purgatory and i say forever will go quicker if we talk you know the winter trees into shivering the nonexistent wind i'm shortening my days in an odd lyricism of unnecessary movement you crave wrists and ankle bones and what is it like to feel needed not by someone but by the whole there are no disparities though just i am tired and cannot sleep

spring snow:
spring snow: white magic absorbed into the colour green which is not
any longer the green colour but a denseness in the sunlight

spring snow: we tell the foreign city mad poetry, three homeless share
a bag of chips in the canal tunnel, unkempt, dirty mattress, a tourist
applauds

spring snow: remember when i deigned to hold your hand and now
she's an aftermath
of what was not meant to be

spring snow: god's little affair is done now, he's just blushing away
into rose and his
lilac blue fingertips pulled cumulus over his face- him, like a boy in
love.

spring snow: she said, the heavenly host were like those deeply in
love which implies that they were not those deeply in love in this
spring morning when there's no one around, like a spring when there's
no one and no sound but someone singing out in between the colours
of dawn when there's no one around but me.

spring snow, you were meant to be
real.

<u>clasped fingers</u>
afterwards, i realized that you had proposed
which was funny because i didn't remember
when you could last stand to be near me.
it never need happen.
your love was a fawn stumbling through the brush at snowy nightfall,
dew splotched.
i'm so tired i can hear your voice to my ear.
unkissed, i know we have something to live for.

<u>all these angels breathing through the strange silent film of life:</u>
why does your fairy child hate me so much she has a precious stillborn
heart and a tendency to drift away it is like walking in a feeling wood
at first light the saplings trembling and nothing at all unthawed i'd do
anything and she'd be nothing, easy, god is here, wandering through
the nether and refusing to be seen

<u>before the fall,</u>
the sky in a lilac rose before it falls,
scatter the winter trees.
until quick the blue shroud
pulled over the earth and all of us under
expiring the breath of our bodies
into a dulled omnipotence.
maybe souls glow low in the beckoning
night shudders.
if this were a love note for you, it would get
lost in the ambiguity. but
it is a comparison darkness. if this were a letter
sent by sea,
it would be lost,
no one would ever read. a terrible and immersive blue.
it has me gone and nebulous.
but i can't spell my own
luminescence if this were written to
the moon and all the nighttime cars through the nighttime roads,
headlight countryside,
the plummeting.
you're the only one in the dark
enough to make light.

everywhere i go i hear her crying.
her perfume sticks.
maybe life for her is more careful.
i do not know her, her name, anything. but i know why she cries. i
wish i too could
unleash fair thunderstorms behind closed doors
in the middle of the morning. she is in the nether stall, she is quaking
at the door of her own grown threshold
in the midst of life.
four steps away, i am always
kept by her exultations these they sound
as though she were dying. and then sometimes there is someone
playing the piano altogether loudly. there are many pianos being
played at once but
i am sitting in a room of older people
and there is nothing more comforting.
am i the one who should be
imprisoned in white until i rest.
death just moss musical on the rocks, hardly an aftermath,
a new caught distance between stars
when it may not be raining. of my universe to yours,
a blessing fell out.

<u>i'm sad that you cut your hair</u>
i remember how it was full of care dark dense.
the storm gathered itself up and left.
did the fierce life of your body undo itself
easy i think the plummet. is it somewhere, the locks i mean
but i could not care for them

still, i think, somewhere your loss degrades. maybe it soils a floor.
probably, the wind.
the wind, probably blows you quickly nowhere, you, a nothing, into
nowhere. i think of you often

i think of the blue under the bridges when i think of you i think of how
bay grips the mind of sky and pulls under, us, into a gravity
as you lose, as by falling, loss, as by
and in falling, there a simple suicide. a blue smear against
i'm sad that you cut your hair.

surely it must be somewhere, your loss hidden underneath a stairwell i
hope where sunlight steps carefully through the afternoon and no one
has to be anywhere,
i mourn your hair quietly all through the daylight hours i sit still in the
staircase and tread nothing and bathe myself with bare hands and no
water in the waterfall-ing of great light, of a simple god looking down
and smiling an unknowable smile but now i mean

the misery of an omnipotence that is no one
and he is no one. so where are you?

we are all gentle no ones treading or tossing because i remember how
like a sea
it was when i craved to move fingers through the terrible quivering
skiffs
destined for no place. i remember that night
when against the timbers we roamed motionless and you motionful,
cupped yourself in your own hands
and i held you tight, inward, as though you might implode, a little star
done in on itself all at once,
dying in rapturous light but then just a soft sigh of incandesce into the
heavens.
you exhale, i respire. i hold no one. he is a cold body at dusk and
his hair cropped close and dull against the neck of him, the

always again i find you dying and then must save no body and i cannot
even save no body so
i close your dead eyes and walk into a black, close night.

blue curve ii.

it's not true love, not even the first on the page. she's another body stripped down in the snow beauteous and ignoramus, probably just sleeping. the whole world off. prone. to lie. that i pour. all: of compassion into/i am is losing.

they live like they: will not die/take it all for granted or just take it all or just take it.

they all love like: they do not love.

i live like: i loved so much, fighting not to plummet from window and fall into the shaped snow shadow;

the only emotion is landscape without tracing the blue curves of catskills, like the hudson breaking apart its organism as sheets of dead ice commit. suicide into the february water, each a contained sky to pull us into our own. at least believe the land. there is no outlasting this, the people you really love will never.

<u>that is being the beating the heart</u> beating an earth feeling the terrible cosmic reason the "you fall in love with everything and nothing" /// to be ruthless and stubborn and mindless and terrible and have no comfort or grounding of the earth, heedless! but this is human useless, this is a deadening, a forgetting of what it is that is important what it is we are doing with these little lives, who cares of sacrament but don't say you care of something and then shrink and shrink and expect me to do nothing when you know what i have professed (this is not of you for you) and what you have and when you lie naked under the stars-

when i was a little thing, i'd sit over the baseball field in the afterdusk and contemplate the dust with
the wise little eyes i had then but whenever a body came over the fence
i turned away and against the sun (it was the moon i loved best).
everyone was so enchanted
and nobody cared to know anyone which was the best thing because i was the only one and then there was the whole
universe to myself until a child came by and i decided then never to speak to him
which was like leaving an apple out on the countertop overnight and never remembering to come back for it
while falling into a senseless dream.

and so i dreamt of her and maybe it was the first time to think of being so close as to inhale the nothing of her hair and face for really she is not there and that is why i am alright with being close, bending sunshine into sweetness and having no thirst.
now i think of you needing me rarely like a strange creature the terrors of your spine and so much nothing i can do for you about it's every caring translated into the smallest of you if only it had been like how people "meet" each other, no this is terrible. it is me being me and you being you if only we could be thrown away easily and i don't know and i don't know what will happen maybe i really can end it and maybe i already have but then i think well maybe the world will turn again, you will go back home or whenever something happens that unsettles your life again and gives you a moment alone to think and need something, an anchor, you will return
and the whole wretched thing will cycle over.

the ghosts are rising.
i forget beautiful things.
my spine's ripped in nonsense,
spring so sweet it could be sound.
the bay will serve as shroud
over my dead bones. faithlessness was an easy way to go,

it did not mean burning, it meant waking
into the world. i am made.
it keeps
me as surrender was comforting. i miss her
even in the light of day. i'm sorry.

we were all afraid somehow
but the people are still attached to their own souls.

<u>the snow</u>
here is something of the snow:
there is nothing soft in the snow,
only the bodies to be taken up
with one
arm and held over the back. to lift
them to their heaven places but without
touching for they are immaculate
and what it means to be ruinous.
what it means to be ruined and silent
and vacantly sitting in the snow hoping
to freeze to death
so i try to keep. because
there is a heart in the isle and i don't know anything but that it
sits in the hollow of the earth and holds the cosmos up.

there is nothing of the snow:
i don't feel anything of it.
to be afraid, is to lie prone
or to not lie but to destroy everything
and everyone we ever cared for?
i have a light for you but only of me.
but that is too. i want to get as close to nothing
as possible near you
in my vacant bones, thoughtless dead-eyed
nobody walking through the midnight snow tasting its universe.
i'm going to be here
anyway to really know a thing
for what it is, a thawing beauty
of nothing landscape especially
when wandering in the full daylight dark
of a mind but i am spectre only
of what it was, a
little luminescing thing or a soul.

analogies

the black ocean under the beating moon before the afterdeath feeling of the soul when i see you and think nothing of seeing you.

part two is like a brief meandering through a mind that must not be your own but still that you inhabit and know.

being is like a song if you like to sing and do it well but only when you're in your room alone and not expecting anybody nor even trying to pass the time.

the boy was happy to be dancing naked because he always was so naked amongst the stars and this was easier he thought than dressing for false weather when the night was to him so dark and still.

we traveled far but could find no finite spaces. i touched a finger to my sternum and felt the wasted beat like a moth's wing held in fire.

i wanted you to imagine what it was i was saying without me saying it aloud because i was as close to nothing as possible when i lay beside you and there was nothing to be afraid of anymore.

in the last part of the story, we went into the wood as it darkened and a rain began to fall that didn't reach our skin but fell through the air and buried in the leaves and soil and into something indistinguishable that we dreamed to be the soul of the land or the heart of us as it came into being.

we were consequently resurrected long enough to listen to bad jazz and sit in a triangle with kind people to talk about the discrepancies of life in a room that had been pulled clean of its clever adornments and taken up only by a host of christmas lights in the midnight hour that saw us speaking but not drunk at all.

and afterwards, he pulled me into a green dense night when summer had hallowed the heavens and opened up the spaces between the stars until we were borne of a grand wishfulness or perhaps just born enough to wander the earth emotionful and neglected by the unspoken spaces of ourselves.

so i went into a white building and carved a word into my wrist but very gently with a small knife that somebody had left there and afterwards i admired the scratched letters under the streetlight and hoped that they would fade but not so quickly as if they had never been.

i just have a whole universe of compassion for you.

<u>i'm doing laundry in my head</u>
look at you not looking at me i open the windows and close the night air,
its steaming cricket song and after-rain drivel away,
i go into the bathroom and wash my face and go out of the bathroom and
i go into the bathroom and wash my face and go out of the bathroom and
i go into the bathroom and wash my face and go out of the bathroom and
i go into the bathroom and wash my face and go out of the bathroom and
you go into the bathroom and wash your face and go out of the bathroom
and i go into my room and see you there but you are not there.
you wash your face, you wash your face, you wash your face, you
put on your boots and walk out and you are still walking out in this
static episode of real life a broken t.v. set when you're sick and sleepless and living in
an album that circles round and sounds like someone else's life in black and white
and you
are still folded into my cloud and that is a terrible dream that paralyzes my larynx and unhinges my
intellect and drives a caged bird out
into a sad strange night when the stars so burning bright
do not reach the other stars with constant light,
knowing only the black brimming holes of empty space that is a cruel and beautiful trance of listening to also
your caged bird and you
breathing and the slanted annotations that life has created on your illiterate frame, the way your bones sometimes
feel warm
because this is autumn, the only time when i hold the moon in my hand
but no, instead i am easily powerless and dangerous
-ly proud of it and you are a fallen
angel or "whatever you want me to be" or just a kid in the dark sung out of his nighttime heart,
lost at sea. i only know how to do one thing so here
are your pointless stupid wasted flowers.

i realized at three in the afternoon that the world wasn't coming to an end so
me and my mental rain and my jar of shame, like lightning bugs unclaimed
so quietly dying went to sit on the porch and think about life's little riptide. you ring a bell in my bones-
i'm reluctant to say why unless it's "the brief spell of the moon" like a hollowed orb-
which are alone but have learned
to take up space for the hour that is today. like here is a child asleep here are the golden empires toppled so easily
but he can't speak
as carefully as i might speak
and outside the rumpled clouds above and the mountains plummeting their contrary height into the sky, and fall's warm sleepy uproar.
i open the window and beckon
the world in as i am barely breathing
until the ladybugs in electric chorus of wings
alight
on my every pore, my strangeness of skin. world- ravaged, you bring bitter black universes to my lip in sweetest sufferings.
as if an alabaster boy were smoking outside my window, i am a vast midnight held in by an empty room of contour.
i was named for light but not the light of lights.

<u>i found the heart of the old dim</u>
church basement there was one light bulb and a place for a wrinkling
and then the floor like

the floor of the one room in sachsenhausen camp that made you feel
something not the oven room but the place they took after,
the bodies, and split them. something about the tile, you said
there was no blood, so you walked the wall

and we walked out again only we weren't holding hands i was alone
on the vacant rim of berlin, a whole city balanced under cloud and
barely so i took the sbahn back to the place where no one knew
and lived there for awhile always looking for a body of water to bury
the body of my body in the body
until we had fallen

asleep dreaming of skin-knuckle-skin and you whispered roses to me
in the midst of rems
but still i was distracted by the wide minutia slipping through my
brain.

still a child wading into cold shallows
at the sea shore but more likely unborn shivers from a wind blowing
from the world before this one.

meantime, my entire life is a house party thrown by my butterfly wing
translucent blonde best friend and she says, of course you're invited
and i say,
i'm sorry, i can't come i'm three states away and the party was two
years ago if you think hard enough
your whole

life has already happened, even the sunlit spiraling out, you could sail
it beloved and wander the earth too. you could strike the little stars
dead pretending
the days through their sorry ends

into i, just standing in the
crypt holds you up
like a lover and grips your fragile organs so desperate tight you can't
feel a
thing. i'm trying to remember but

what you don't know is
i'm just a bad metaphor for a light that never goes out.

the story of how you lost all faith in yourself:
your mother didn't take the pills on purpose
or the ambulance was actually coming for you.
some new thing of light you will fall for, she also
will go home to white wards to be held in
her own nothingness
and afterwards be obliterated gently by the hand of god.

it snowed once in berlin
in the springtime when
every island was supposed to have meaning
especially the island of peacocks
but more so, the isle of belles.
you took the train but never got off.

you said you needed to be flung to the cape of the largest
continent. all you found there were ostriches. carefully,
you walked round them, averted yourself, your gaze,
the dim thunder of the surf. later, you'd tell them
the greatest thing was the obliteration of sound
when you fell into the collision of two oceans,
midwinter in africa. it was a yelling kind of frigid,
your whole body syncopated.

eating was difficult because you never wanted the comforts
of the earth, only its ravishments. you ate a heart out of its mind.
and all there was to do was to run down to the train tracks,
jump into the body, knowing

these too are lies, everything you have fallen
for, is also, too, your own.

these days, the earth holds you in grand indifference.
the night sky no longer surrenders itself
into you. (or you into it?)

you never wanted to be loved.

<u>to be</u>
the something of the waterfall is like the poetry of forgetting you or
how the sun falls and all the world under
that time the boy looked too long into my eyes
and found something. and i felt it was best forgotten. i never get
lonesome in the wood.
and when the sun falls and the moon and as stars,
we might enter into the unknown.

i needed a means of forgetting
my soul or to go to the crossroads where it had been taken. i wanted
someone else's jacket
and for the portraits to be returned after the people had died. i had to
rest the lavender before the fall. please only cry when we come to the
garden in the clouds, taste the sky like sweet water with our eyes.

i know there was a shroud pulled over the sky as we were entering into
another world. so i, in the rain, was ruining, bitten as the elderberries.
absently you seized me, clouded as you were by fragments of sky
obscured in the bone. candles burnt to ashes and i am so shy as
shadows hoping to cause no harm. though i am sorry. for the universe
of compassion i have for you. a light in me i know.

i'm lost in a wood at nightfall, a sun burning into my mind, what is this
creekbed running into my head, a field of mint where i go to confuse
the time the sky in lilac forgets the clouds and the colors fall into a
dusky dream and i too die as the sun dies into me like a soft
reverberating song with no end which is like the presence of a dim and
unlikely universe by which i am possessed or i am the embodied of it
as, a body, i sink into the stream and not wakefully rise sullen through
the rapids, another stolen shape out of the cosmic ache into that dark
ceaseless that awaits, that is, eternity.

i confess, once again i've fallen in love with the unknown.
it was early morning, not all of the nocturnal things had hidden into
the sprawl of bush, nor even the light had gained its somethingness, no,
it was plaintive, still as you or i in the breath of the dawn not yet
exhaled. i did not reach for you then, i knew you were just a dream.

so dawn bit the throat of me breathing and my nested ribs unearthed i
was dragged from the buried ground, i was graceless and sick at heart
and thrust into the clouds like a sullen moon to haunt the light of day.

you held my hand in the noon. i was dim and paralyzed, my heart like
an impassive sky as it is held in quarry water. i was feeling the how of
everything as the lakes and rivers rippled in heavens all under me.

your voice broke with fear when you said i love you. and i couldn't
trace the contour of your being any longer and the awe of you fell out
like a casual vacancy. or unhealable sorrow. the cosmic ache that was
once you.

<u>I'm missing your moon.</u>
By then, of course, we weren't speaking again, which was alright but for my silent distractedness late at night when I became convinced that myself was just another storm to be weathered and the trees sighed all through the early morning hours and I turned and I turned and there was no one there so I was borne aloft in dead ocean of dreaming that filled the vacant spaces of the empty house and I knew all at once that I was nothing as could be held by the wide earth.

But you can hold the sun in your hand at this hour, look, and he looks and raises his wrist and cups the sun and he says to me, you know you're all I got, and I said, no, there's this everlasting light, see, just beyond the window and so infinite, and you're holding onto it, you're holding onto infinity, like, I don't know.

damn, they took you to the spirit realm.
scraps of sky starry what is it like to be forgotten and how do i get
there today. these strangers are breathing my breathing back into their
breathing the trees sneezing in a not yet autumn wind, the alien
diaspora is contemplating going home.

to be the heart i am no longer subordinate to the idea of myself. the
vultures have dragged me into the wood to celebrate in blossoming
scarlet and pus. and to unthread the delicate architecture of my spine.
the night is gentle and my echoed breath forms hardly a sound as i
tread gently on the unknowns and death comes to take my hand and
kiss my neck so my brokenness slips through the cracks into the is
there another world? in the universe, there are beautiful things.

that is, to give a word to the feeling in the afterdark to feel every
breathing part of my body the freight consumed me in a sound and the
sky took me up in its color i did not think of anything then, no, the
earth was a blessing. it is love just to know that you exist somewhere.

<u>Oh so you can be?</u> So you can be hallowed and strange in your abscesses, the rifts in your somebody else's sweater but I forget you are living somebody's life and I am not here but another casual vacancy is I dream too sweetly of nothing this is what the dead are made of these laceless silences and the way you move which is a yawn in the universe, which is awe, which is cosmic oh and could you be? I do not. I do not work here and it is not my birthday and I will not eat the plum cake from the nice girl because you have my silhouettes in your eyes and this terrifies me to think I might've hurt you I might be hurting you and the pain is to stretch a skeleton against the earth and beat you into it like a heart that lost its. The heart never loses anything and you are okay, you are not looking for a book, you are in the library, you speak audibly in no one's voice and I wish you were unrecognizable but you are not but for the way you move which is traumatic to think of how you moved all through the halflit unwaking hours in the basement of your house next to the blind cat and next to me whispering nothings in between your bones and no one could catch them, no. Being near you was apocalypse and I was an apology unto your corpse when you left I planted so many flowers all over my own spine and buried my head into the ground. I would like very much to see your blood to know you still have it in you, anything. Or to hear you breathe like you meant it and still knew you were alive as you were walking through the dark wood. Are you dreamless? Is that you I hear in the dark? No, I have no reason for you. It was the logic of your vertebrae, it was the mind of your heart. Yes, I really mind you. Yes, I really wanted to save you. But no longer, and then longer, and then the moon. If it is you that I am hurting, I will bury my own bones so you will not have to see them. But that is not true because I am a regardless and there is a vacancy between me and your glass eyes and it never goes away and I must, I must go carve a word into my hand or else to look away. The people say to look away. I do, and I fall into a stupor, I fall into an ocean of dreaming and never wake and I dance across the voids and know what it is to be luminescent there is something tragic between us in that you cannot acknowledge it and it doesn't go away (but I wish it were to go away).

To think that I can never make you feel okay.

grocery shopping/i am distraught

death is not at all in opposition to life i went grocery shopping and i needed to buy an apple not to eat to buy an apple because this is an example of an idea i had when i was grocery shopping to buy an apple but just because i was buying an apple (not to eat, for the idea) i decided not to buy the cheese because the apple and the cheese are two very different things and the absence of life is not necessarily death

i went to a grocery store with an imaginary boy let's call him jack, jack and i went to the grocery store and jack started to cry in the frozen goods section but we don't know why. neither jack nor i know why he began to cry in the aisle next to the frozen peas. i looked at him and i said, well i don't want to get you down i don't want to get anyone down and that is what got him down, so to speak, but i hadn't said anything and the boy wasn't crying so we went to buy some milk because that is after all, what we came to the store to buy.

i got very tired one day and i didn't get up and nothing happened. the postman woke and he delivered on the other side of the door and the small animals crept around the spaces of the house and the cats raised their hackles about the neighborhood and a man spraying the fresh concrete shouted up at the sky that it was all done and painted but he wasn't talking to god he was talking to another man and three old women in white stood outside a catholic church and talked in a very minute and particular way about very lovely small things and they grew closer and closer about the virgin mary and i didn't get up and then the sun fell through the windows and cracks in my house (and through the cracks in my eyes, the cracks in my skull perhaps to penetrate some strange and ancient heart like an unlikely universe tucked in the darkening but this was not so and this was not so and this was not

we didn't buy anything at the grocery store. we drove there and jack wandered through the aisles singing about someone who had died and i slipped a block of cheese into my bag and then we both walked out and didn't say anything and a woman who worked there came up to us to wish us a nice day and jack said yes, it is a very nice day in fact though jack didn't know yet that he didn't exist and that i made him up merely for the purpose of detailing this brief and entirely fictional episode which is also so pointless) because in fact, i had never gotten up, though i was wide awake i dreamed through the hours in a dark and i thought i was dying and it was true, i was dying and i thought i was living, and it was true, there was nothing more horrifying.

<u>words don't mean anything</u>
i think there are things that you may not understand about me, there
are times when i am alone in the dark and it is very cold- i do not think
you understand- it is very cold.

i know i make it hard, i know i'm distant and strange and quiet and
intense and it's hard to fit anywhere real, and i'm sorry because i want
to be quiet old friends with you, i want to talk to you sometimes but
not other times, i want there to be nothing that you are afraid of
between us. i seek the wordless peace. but even if that is a possibility,

i cannot imagine many things worse than my care for you being
something that makes you feel weighted in any way

sometimes i miss you the most when i'm around you, i have much
missing for the whole cosmos, and also some for you in particular, is
horrendous but that is how i exist and there is exaltation in that

freedom is basically nothing anyway
yet in the heart, a greatest feeling
the distress of an uncapturable soul

i have many vivid imaginings. not all of them are my trying to
recollect the contour of your face elusive as the line of mountain and
sky, i like the angles of you and even the fixed points, these as they
shift and mesmerize. i am obsessed with every incarnation of your
sweet terrible form.

we've known each other since before we were born.
i miss you. but i'm right here.
i'll always love you.
you're so familiar. you're so familiar too.
you're the most beautiful thing i've ever seen.
too much because you're perfect.
i just wanted to be alone.

i like new york city only in the hour when the sun is setting and in
forgetting, how the sun still gives in upon us everlasting light.

it was the only time that i realized that your face could be ugly, with
your lips flared back and your eyes inscrutable but small, so small, and
your nose twisted into something, it was remarkable, truly i had no
feeling but for

the feeling of something beautiful falling away.

still, there was an eternity to your look. i did not want to forgive it, my soul was unrelenting, still there was the old oblivion.

i like the cracks in your ceiling and the dawn chilling the walls in a green splendor before we return to the heart of the gold glad of this thing beating, that is, the ceaseless miracle of you existing at all

i am thinking of the light of you.

<u>i thought it would be funny to run to the end of the earth</u>: there was nothing there to interest me. i tried throwing myself off but this was like not finding the thing you were looking for. this was like finding ghosts in a newly built house. this was like forgetting who it was you were or who your soul had been sold to. this was like trying to find your imaginary brother in the woods where he liked to go before he died. everything was so terribly beautiful and I had no idea what was happening. this was like realizing you cared an awful lot about the cosmos and all that but you weren't sure you could attach any importance to the feeling or indeed to anything.

<u>meetings with dead things</u>
it is strange that it is sentience the creature hit
just lifted in an eternal grimace of impact.
should i recognize the pain that is my pain, pull
lavender flowers from the earth to place on the breast of the animal.
(after i push the dead cat gently to one side of the road
feeling in my gut even its prolonged weight, the way the
body unbending moves as a stricken whole i cannot catch breath
enough
for the unknown creature my heart is shuttered.) still
i do not know myself of moments before, that consciousness
of another form too is extinguished, therefore
i have died, am dead and
alive enough not to know what quite to mourn
except how the universe is scattered in yours and mine chest.

<u>the tunnel of green</u>
upon, walking in the wood alone a greener darkness and a tunnel, she
said a tunnel of green
the water from the fountain of youth tastes like sulfur some days and
other days it does not
the digitized infrastructure of our backwards and forwards
development is just another phantom of the frenzied circle
a dream alone in the blue rooftop blurred by the light of the moon and
the window apertures to keep the temperatures stacked to a heavenly
sky
a thought of who you might be if you weren't thinking so loud in the
dark
it is good, forgetting, but not because it makes way for some other
thing. that is, if everything is eternally existing, and not-
to be washed in a river and taken up else you wouldn't break surface
panting and panic-stricken with lethean tears and a the-universe-fell-
into-me smile
sky washed me up it is kind of like a feeling of
how the rain filled the sky with noncolor and inundated the streets in a
realness
the world made ready to be inhabited by us, the ghosts
to have nothing
i'm sorry that you died the other day but does it feel like anything?
it was just another moment in wondering how the dead quiet of our
souls happened to be here and on the earth too
all the poets they say go to purgatory so i'll meet you there in a little
while
and if i write you this letter, maybe they'll let me in

vermont

we went to vermont to observe a man who, in being, barebacked, betrayed
that he was a laborer and she said that she liked that his body said it was so.
while the boy who was meant to be in the woods cried because he was leaving her in the parking lot
outside the national guard and then we drove back from vermont.

he went into the woods as we made new living rooms and hung lights and rearranged the artifice of our very separate
and seemingly predestined lives and she said it was a beautiful day and it was a beautiful day
and soon it would be over but for the several motorcyclists as they made their way over the horizon and into the dusk of our lives that were not our lives any longer and i couldn't hold anything in my hands any longer, and the sun grazed my face in its everlasting light as it sunk and sunk and there were large pockets of air sucked in and out of his chest as he sobbed which was not even uncanny, it was normal.

and tragedy was boring, and nothing made sense and we were wrapped like saplings around each other in a dead fog, grown into and out of the earth with only the sullen protestations of ourselves
but i wanted to feel at home when we reached the morgue or onward for the mass burial in an unnamed pit on an island where nobody can feel our unfeelingness, that is
and i have already encountered this, it's true but these days mostly, i am most familiar with the bus station between here and maryland or is it delaware i know it when i see it, it makes my heart swell like a strange ugly beast blindly faltering its way through the orifices of mother earth who lies in coma through the toxic frenzy of our lives and she said it was a beautiful day.

and it was beautiful, i could find you in your house, your bones cracked and uncracked in everlasting light and i could look you in the eye, i could say hello.
i could run myself into the ground or a clear bottomless lake thoughtlessly, with all the world of dreaming held intact though i knew what it was i could not hold anything, not even the dying sun, or the moon as it fades from us as we lose the children of ourselves and so are plunged into ultimate undoing.

to know that you will and have and continue to exist is a miracle were it just a thought i had on a rainy day when i was walking by myself as the sky collected its darkness into a sound that was like quietude or even nakedness. and synonymously, that you and i come to the end it is no question but the barest certainty of my brief and unconscionable soul.

reasons to run away and never return
i run away every day, i tell you and we're in the lemon sunshine your car with the cracked
shift the way the engine sings
noise that once drove us nearly
all the way route ninety-five to get away from
all our past lives and i say i run away every day
only sometimes i call you from the side of the road dripping from my body and you
rise and say something about responsibility and how i am of an age
when i don't need for people to pick me up to prove that they would
pick me up when i need to be picked up when i'm on the side of the
road dripping the fierce life of my body, this which most of us
learn to forget and i say this is untrue.
part of running from is loss of proof, why do we run away why because
we do not know, dear heart and you say,
wrenching the gearshift, don't worry
we're almost home.
okay, i say, but why do we run away?
existence, this was a thing i have few words for but there seems to be less of me in it, so i
remember you and i'm sorry to remember you because
you i love to the moon, so i ran
away to the moon and never never
came home at all, did i, dear
heart and where is my heart?
found in so many things of the earth, or how
the wind sighs into us and we know one day
that we will grow old and then we will die.
there are many things one cannot run from,
but how we might try
to subtract our known from the unknown and
dismantle the universe's arithmetic i wish
you knew me like i know you but it's hapless,
this. so i go, i run away again
and this time into the sun
like maybe that perfect day that ran away, that wild summer's day, that dance in the space
before death was something wiser
than i because i felt it in my chest and it said to me,
this is what it said: you run for the departed
devotions, how would you know it as love
until it's been lost?

the spirit realm
october snow: i wanted to pretend i was writing you a letter so i could
rip it up spread it gather wind around every refrain so forlorn until the
meanings flew up into the landscape of autumnal dreaming and i
could catch shatterings of heaven on my tongue

i am raw cold tetherless i think of you:
we were sitting under a heavy lavender sky with the wind and rain
talking and crosslegged, facing each other, heads together to listen to
guitar riffs and later i listened to his breathing and he smelled like
tablecloths newly washed and put out to dry on old tree branches
husked and worn by long autumn
you are looking into the inside of the world but haven't learned to
speak about it. you don't want to. you are far easier to be around than
anyone else. i want to be a friend and i am afraid of breaking this
heavy lavender sky into more meanings than the world contains in its
distant dreaming mind

how to get to the spirit realm:
go to a place of unwholesome dreaming
realize that your dreams are this place and the people you see in them
are real.
wake at strange hours to run into the woods. either at dusk or dawn as
the landscape blurs into itself and the sun burns like a pyre.
care deeply for all the glowing earth. the air is thick with ghosts
moving in and out of themselves. be also unmoved.
you will be drawn to places full of ghosts. when people ask you what
it is like in the spirit realm. you will say it is no different from the real
world they know. everything is eternal and you are not afraid. both life
and death appear mild. there is no way of getting to the spirit realm.
you must find your own way of getting there yourself. you are
probably already there but are not yet aware.

and upon entering the spirit realm:
and in discovering a universe
you are sleepy and tousled not hard to find
with small ribs and a gentle outline
and i am lost somewhere not here
in an odd omnipotence as though i were quite unintentionally
becoming one with the wind, that is, the sleepy rainy october sky as
the leaves plummet in gentle never-ending suicide.
the angels came down from heaven and lifted my body into the air:
i am becoming a ghost uncertainly and not really with a thought in my
mind the woods turned a blue so deep the earth was no longer a color
but rather a feeling of itself, the pale exhalation of surrender is what
keeps me if i am indeed alive just as i-
thank you for coming to my bedside earlier today in great white light

everlasting, to know that you are here forever is no unbearable
burden…i saw an angel of you and of me too.
i fell upwards as one with the sky in light and light and light

<u>here is some cosmic amnesia to keep us tied to our present earthly processes</u>
in the process of forgetting you i have found a world of beauty, though last winter you were closer than you ever had been, it is february again- separately, we watched the ice crack along the river and i did not miss you so much then because you were there, in a way, unrelenting. i trusted you to carry my dead body to the sea in your own hands and set fire to that small craft of evergreen until even my corpse was set free.

now you are awash in sunlight- i do not want to be near you but i want to know how near i am to your terrible heart. there is always another way of how i might forget you.

i hope you are sad only in the good foreign ways, cosmically, in the shower or upon the suddenness of waking beneath a cracked ceiling, yes, there is always something of you in these finite linear bends of the endearments of how you navigate your brief absurd temporality, these are not only astonishing to me but wholly infinite in that i love you though perhaps it would be better

if I had never recognized you when I first saw you

it is getting so cold, between us. i think the winter will be the end, of me anyway. until the sun pools out across the ice sheets. we fall upon a gold stillness.

<u>something</u>
no i wouldn′t say i love you because there's no noble potency to it, no divine except for
the power of softly, being.
teach me cautiousness, yours specifically
and i will say, do not be afraid but it is no use
you say we are two very different kinds of people
and i say, well i am fond
of you and you say nothing but hold my bones in your bones when it is snowing in october
it was easy losing you, sweet- utter sadness
obscured in white drifts, a dim universe.

<u>new winter</u>
i woke empty as a cloud drawn out in soft lines about an
underwhelming sky. you used to crack when you were close to me like
a frail unbendable twigged winter tree, i wanted to know
your seizures of the heavenly light between broken branch and limb as
you were frightened in the wind. last night i sought to apologize again
for some unnamed things i did. hurts i cannot remember. lances of
light shivering from an open window i lie
motionful and unable to commit my bones to anything. i am more and
more
just a slivered form posted like a crescent moon as she dies
exhales her lisped white into an ancient
darkness. oblivion means less than it used to and i am ready at any
moment to be dying.
your phone did not even ring and this was a relief in a way
that i do not have to leave the white room on the third floor above the
root cellar
where the kid musicians moan their adolescent soliloquies into the
marked floorboards
and into the everlasting blue star-strewn. i remember that time we sat
on the fire escape and you spilled hot water
stories below and it was unremarkable. we were quick accidents, even
your dark eyes.
and when i unearthed the body from the frozen earth,
pulled from the drift and kissed only by my wish
to make the world good to you. this was incidental. you were only
another sleeping form lapsed into the snow in complete erasure.

<u>fables</u>

i. this is a fable about a boy and a girl and
the boy is not inside of a room but neither
is the girl and this is a different thing because the girl is not inside of
anything
while the boy is just not inside of a room: my new pastime is lying
face down in large crowds of people and listening to ankles shivering
by the scent of their personal arrangements life of electric veins

ii. a sleepless dream that you were here mere moving static on t.v. in
white rooms my new favorite hour is waiting senselessly for life to
catch up with me is to die minutely and soundlessly in a field with the
stars out and sad love songs in earbuds

iii. remember when your skin nocturnal seashell remember moonlight
through windows don't check hold your dreams under the pillowcase
and keep them when you were here remember you

iv. sketching vases graphite for the empty spaces literature under the
bones ''love is a lonely thing'' on canvas no one has words anymore i
wake up and wash my face you wash your face empty rooms amazing
how empty rooms you walk into

v. this is a fable about a boy and a girl but it's not really about a boy or
a girl it's just about ten minutes watching the sky turn green in
predawn respiration of the sun and how pendulum the heart sings and
something about how we were made but mostly about how we can't
remember how we were made

AND THE LIGHTS GO OUT IN THE MIDDLE OF THE NIGHT

dearly;

don't. everyone is. i think gone even without a word. i live in a ghost
town wandering through memory for rainy eternity. a dream that girl
led for a briefest spell but all is done now, one drenching anonymous
day and spirits reclaim it all. this is for your dead wasted heart this is
for your endlessly raining bones this is a song that has yet to begin,
never grew its wings crippled bird won't you rise over the horizon

don't forget yourself so softly like a child crying into the cloud sheets
don't your vertebrate cry for undoing or was that a dream too real for
this one or how many perfect days could I condense in vowel sounds
that resound in my walk, the smallest ringing conversation of my
bones against each other, veins flowering like winter things caught in
new year's frost, maybe these hours are shirts hung on the clothesline
in a rainstorm, not meant to dry maybe i'm not meant to be alive
yet i have so much nothing and you have so much nothing must you
bring the bitterest imaginings to me in the space of an hour you look
like you've fallen off a watchtower too much being in your bones
makes you shiver from unwarm, the frail flowers of your heart
growing so barely
and a fatal poem face, your blossoming paleness, nose frozen and
fixed
lips, eyes shivering sailing ships embedded in a profound arctic,
you turn your head and i
turn the lights out and i
don't let this place forget, i grant a nonsense
of darkness, ground the halls in unreality and let the ghosts in
to run naked, no one can observe the barest spirit now,
there is no one here because there is no one
to be seen except to unalign the sleepy exit signs
and you turn your head and you
turn your head and you
say sorry, a demure child of an apology, maybe
a little wavering boy neglected outside, or that desperate
thank you running to and fro always needing to be alone. only fear-
you aren't being
kind, you're in so many pieces and i know
all of them like the skeleton of the god who made me and you
and forgot everyone else- leaves you naked and terrible: "i'm just me,
wherever you want me
to be". i say the moon to you

like,
i have this great feeling for you.
like,
i really don't mean to hurt you here all these things i said
when i thought you were sleeping were true but i didn't mean for you
to hear them.

<u>consequence</u>
must I only be a body when I undo the screen and open (pour the night air in)
a window? the horizon enthralls those
dull eyes. I aspire to be lifeless, to move
only through a midnight grass and from
bus stop to bus stop through the sinking hours of the moon and a deadweight sun
rocking its little ship through starry morass.
I am in so many places at once and I know none of them. I am brushing the clouds out of my hair and wishing you were here because you kept the moon in your sleeve and the sun under your tongue I have been dreaming of dying not in the large ways but merely dipping back into the bays, their deep bodies of water and thinking of the profundities of small bodies enveloped openly by nothing but this is a strange story with no emphasis because you dot the empty halls with commas and keep syntax to yourself when really I am so empty it is like you could pull the universe right out of me.

i shaved my head and i didn't know why and i didn't know
so i didn't speak to anybody
except for the sun who was kind.

i went into the church to lie down and
i tried my best to demonize myself.
it was like something beautiful that happens every day
a sunrise but it's so tiring to go on about.

he wants to know when i will tire of his weaknesses these that pale his
skin and make him shake like winter trees and are so
like the cracking of the ice floes and the contour lines of the
nonexistent mountainside and all the world that is an unrelenting
miracle and i said no

i cannot tire except in the miseries of my perpetual to feel what it is i
am feeling and to know of a spiritual gold or thing called the soul and
to know what it is we are being no

and will i scare you off someday or will always you wander
unbeknownst
or always will you seek a great unknown
though i seek a great unknown to wrap me up in its terrible crucifix
and drive me
so mad but you do not twitch, you smile a slow
and this is a dark appreciation of the things we are knowing and what
it means

to be together but alone, or the great fear of being as traipses petals
through the garden of love in the afterdark and a sunk blue moon to
quiet the neverminds and the
i miss you.

i fall for the contour of the catskills and the ice cracking in your spine
because your shivers are impassive and will never care for me at all.
oblivion is here all the time now and it's very calm.

nobody goes to hell. there is only a remorseful god washing the dead
in holy water.

i.

early morning
the pearly "forget me"s of the cirrus wound through struck star
and the sun still sleeping. in this, i pray for you inaudibly,
prayers that catch on the hem of my sleeve as i kneel
to bathe the bodies in holy water.

ii.

to bathe the dead, you must know
the first luminosities of their skin
so you do not wash out the somethingnesses
once held in and out.

iii.

you said to forget you so that you could forget yourself
more easily. i fall asleep so easily
when i am alone in an infinite dark. now
in the hauntings of the dark, where lonely the god walks,
i am glad to erase your finite bends,
the careless care of your body
just possessed by a dream. there was no you in it.

<u>the only thing</u>

i.
i'm losing it, the butterfly moments, the singing verdant greens of the
nighttime grasses in the
aftermath of you i retire to my pretty chapel
a boy walks in, he says- but would you mind
if i? i say i would not mind and then there is the liquid architecture of
the organ as he plays, for nobody. he is practicing,
i am practicing in all the smallest ways of me like how the clouds are
just a different symmetry every day in the pale
absorption of sky, the pale absorption of you, your pretty face, your
sweet chapel eyes,
a terrible organ inside, the dull beating heart
that sings for nobody.
because, in the end, we are what we are, because in the end,

the sun lowers us into a momentous oblivion. in the end,
i lose you and i lose me too and
i don't even care.

ii.
open your eyes. we are in a new
place. you tell me, slowly, that you have died
or are dying. i say nothing. i hold your hand and pull you into the
beyond. you don't mind. nobody minds, except for the scintillating
moment in time, a brief human dream of us before it's all over and you
open your eyes, tight little
universes inside, already asking me-
who will close my eyes when i die? and i say, nobody,
nobody but me.

iii.
nobody is a harsh body in a windstorm. i think of you often,
my whole life through. i think of the beneath the cliff
when i think of you. it is the most of anything i have ever known. it is
impact,
it is reaching into a beautiful oblivion when i am
only what i am.
nobody walking through the sleeping people.
a sky of repose. i leave you
as quickly as i can. i never forget,
still-

i stole away into a pleasant darkness. i embraced the illusion of the
world.
i embraced you, late at night. your deadly idea.

i only cared for things.
no one could keep the way that you fell asleep. no one could keep
the everlasting chamber of the heart. no one could keep me,
or you. i was tucked, enveloped
in a senseless dream. even the moon was pulled away.
no one could keep love. but it was.

the cape (of good hope)
beneath the dark sloping of mountain and every color in the sky
like a new language descending it's you
i miss but i don't remember who you are
and then all the little lights, their brief lives, the idea
of humankind or a friendly
sort of oblivion still i cannot forget
you. i think of you often. more times than the
changing moon because it's a buried moon,
a light that under it all doesn't go away, you say.
ever, you say. i think of you mostly when i'm deep in sleep

and not thinking any longer, just sunk in a dream of love when dream
is just a word
for the mountains becoming a blue
into the sky while love is just a

we were riding in a car and i forget
where we are going. if i forget
your face, its unbearable landscape, i
won't beg your forgiveness
any more than i would ask favors of the moon or sun. things are just
as they are.
i miss you missing me missing you of the missing moon of the starlit
sun of the wild night in its raging ocean of dead atmosphere and
missing is a word
for
the way you fall asleep.

i can't forget. it was a beautiful evening. we were just coming back
from traveling, from one of the ends of the earth and oceans with the
new names humans have given them. still, under the water, all things
collide. still, we might never have happened upon one another, split
stars and nothing. or nothing. i'm not sure so i dangled my feet over
the edge and didn't for a moment believe that dying was a relief, no,
these things didn't matter much, i was all caught in a dream- for once, i
was in a place.

<u>the real moment</u>
was when the building of summer loomed rectangles large against the
city but
a small palace in the imperceptible
blue background of foothills of nothing and somewhere a dim river
and the columns looming between the unkissed couples,
just figures that momentarily eclipse
one another, in pursuit
of seeing what it is they are seeing
that is beyond them and it is like
something they can't remember but just feel all the time now, wind
blowing through their softly souls,
like brushstrokes pulling them umbiblical-ly to and fro, swifter than
swans wading through the surface of the sky
on the closed fountain and the sun so forever in my hair and on my
skin outline until i know where it is not is myself.

afterwards you said it was
nice for once
to look with someone who could really be with the place.

<u>how to construct a belief system and actually believe in it so as to lead
a well adjusted life</u>
i'm a creature of strange yearnings;
this morning i was like, as if sleep could erase my body and ran to the
most beautiful

house with a waterfall for a front yard and a station wagon that barely
pulls over the
rutted bridge while
the bluebells are frosted their lovely hearts. will i think of you as you
lay dying or will my mind be quieted by the voice of heaven and will i
be bored by it all

rearrangement of the same bones so let's go to the city
and get picked up by strange men and wander off giddy through the
half light or never, never at all forget ourselves

as time goes on drop off the edge of the earth into a clear lake and the
bottom is everlasting- it is your heart and there is nothing more
horrifying we backed the car into a tree
the tree shattered us, we broke apart. a doe ran across the road like a
universe's spare hiccup
remember at all times, you are at random.
or just the logic of your mother or just the algebra of
i am brainless senseless twisted up and gutted piece of astral trash

but i did not leap or toss breath into the bay that is,
it did not my nostrils close me up and heavy the lungs that are
filled finally
the ocean did not consume, that is,
the radioactive waters were made wicked by the perspiring of a
million lightbulbs, the breathing of the households billowing in snow
and hot air all through the winter months
though i have once broken and i have once fallen and i have
very little and nobody

or the lovely sleeping earth. would you move towards me in sleep
again some day
as the stars shatter through an undeniable sky, or well, this is too
wretched. you don't answer
to my voice or desire. the world is fairly
crystalline. this doesn't do it for you.

you're in danger of erasing the stars when you twitch, accidental
meteor showers when you shiver your lips, cheekbones, skin-scarred
in memory)

maybe many things when she lay beneath an impassive sky
so walk with me

i'll miss you even when my light is sputtering out. in all the daily
resurrections, my love for
you is true also and will ruin me and ruin the earth but dearly i hope
not to ruin you.

there was
not a star as could be touched. there was no dark night listening to
your
profession of cosmic love.
the world wasn't listening.

january 2nd to january 3rd was in epochs of bare bones
exposed to morning light and late
time lost itself reckoning against
granted the most sweet traumas of flesh
unto no excess or moved
soon he will be limitless soon i too
even the wintered woods greet me the same
you confessed we were raged
by cosmic imaginings so
i tried to find messages close against your chin while you purred little
dark things
roses down my spine
and measured the slowest of my pulse
though it wasn't new there's no one
but i and in the heart, you
who has miraculous topographies i can't but notice and the closed lips
over the dear face nothing displaced, dark eyes of stillness i can't
forget anything
of you,
i left one cup a teabag inaudible no more to drink the things we
couldn't speak about before
i can't speak of at all

<u>spring theologies</u>
i. the saviour will save you as he has saved all those whom he has
saved who are in the saviour who is like the mother of all those he has
saved and this is an endless god and this is
being consumed by such damning love
ii. i remember mostly the silence you gathered under your breath how
it rimmed my skin in magnificent faithlessness how finally i could
reach out to
what was beyond me,
grapple with far darker infinities
iii. i never could forget your face but what was but a marker of
circumstance, the senseless trance of how i am i
and you are just
always you so softly sleeping like the shrine stones in the graveyard
only we aren't dead yet living is just
such an unsure prospect that is always happening all the time
iv. and my only well of insight was my universe tucked tight against
my chin tell me again about the little hearts of ours so briefly beating

<u>the only emotion is landscape</u>
the indian burial ground was alright
or the limp soft of a cat corpse
i had never

as the docks like a letter to the no rain as one steps off into the
lakes of overflown grey

in a fervor, birds over the wheat field
fling their scrappy bodies into a sinking sky
scars of the world

the way the nowhere land goes
foothills for bodies
houses that sigh into the earth again

and the temperament of the creek as wide as summer passes into a dull
emerald
scintillating an internal cosmos

the glory of a ruined space in cold weather

last autumn frost
the woodland architecture huddled up
into a mind of late autumnal
dreaming,
i cannot remove the lichen bodies
where they dwell in steadfast
frosted epochs
so i buried in the bay and froze my own
terrible bones, thinking of
eyes harder than any eyes
a blacker blue
than beacon soul-shining outright and your pearly nose,
lined lips without miss you
don't care about the rest you just
rise away trailing
your left
whispered hand knowing what it is you know
when we fall upwards into a periwinkle sky
that can't or won't erase
the deadly stars of our fated minds,
held in but alien universes inside.

<u>luminescing</u>
i severed my spleen between
some winter trees, it was something about how they
seized the sky between their branches,
it broke me. blood drops on this white canvas
like a cardinal flying nowhere to nowhere,
it is easy, i have no eyes, these too
will be gone, my lungs vanquished by the mountains,
those dim sentries in their grey chorus
up into the sky. slowly we all learn to breathe out again,
to take in the whole landscape
and then. my veins always knew they were fleeting
pathways the in and out.
but it was when i came upon the others
bodies in the snow unkissed, the useless feeling
they are immaculate,
it was a beautiful morning, i wish i could convince you of it,
i came apart.
now that there is no one around i can bury the corpse,
we will not need to dress her in warm clothes
she will lay silent and unbreathing in the snow.
except that organ i have pried
from my chest as slowly it begins to snow.
you did not understand these burials,
and yet you are here as much as
any other object, shadows
bend in dull proof of radiance
i cannot forget,
and that is why i fall back into the earth,
a heart given to the universe.

<u>the little minotaur is crying.</u> it rained and so it is always raining. you left and so you are always leaving. there are many worlds in which you do not love me so it doesn't matter whether this is one of them. and yet i want the sea. i want to be overcome. maybe i will die on the highest plateau. maybe if we walk through this door now that the world has ended we will find a new world. maybe if i fish your corpse from the river you will remember because we are amnesiacs wandering the world and everything is in every thing, the universe is in you. all that remains is how you remember.

genesis

i.
you are the space, the place that took god's breath away, and the
moment without him, all creation roared into a fabulous chaos before
it forgot itself again, fades and fades, all desperate shades;
miracles are hardly solid. the best thing about them is that one can
hardly believe them. it is a thing called awe that some cannot
remember. it is why we raise
children.

ii.
once i moved like people move and then
did not move again.

iii.
i will forget you haplessly,
moving towards the sea to wash
the blood out of my body,
you are like the lonely god who is the creator of all that is creation,
that is being consumed by such damning love
and everything placed errantly
in the place where it would be
the most. great sorrow in my
deadweight, released i thought if only i
would drown.

iv.
i cannot forget your face i cannot,
that is one thing i cannot forgive
beauty. i am haphazard,
afraid of the lies of my body,
always running into myself.

v.
god had made his most beautiful apologies. every day i am granted the
sweetest
old tragedies, the sun coming
up and wiser all the world in being
new again, bathed in
endless light.

<u>belle isle mythologies</u>
at the end of the path is a little white house.

in the morning, the world is still there and sun risen. the moon was the
one who went missing. we tried forgetting ourselves

but nothing was working. the body only was.

and brief too. in the center of the isle is the heart. the heart was a
quarry broken up

the earth to build something new

long ago. no one can remember what was created. the quarry filled in
water. a bottomless lake to reflect

a cosmic sky. someone named it the soul

and then ran away into a great unknown. the soul had always, from the
very start,

been surrendered.

there is an anything about us,
there is such an infinity of silent
care within you, your mortal tissue
otherworldly, even
there is an indefinite edge to your sinews, your fragile
nerves growing away like desert
trees, flowering into nothing
like how windowpanes suffer the sweet rain i make nonsense i know
but i would nightly dream to caress the skeleton of your thoughts
a landscape of impossible things,
to plateau
and rise again in melancholy
peaks, these that unveil stranger nothings
like rose-puff clouds undying
even as they are tucked away beneath
the incantations of the moon, its unsunk darkness. your psyche
is such a spell i've just been thinking
of how you exclaimed that you couldn't
help but need
to kiss my brain, knowing of all the things it contained
and you didn't know me still
and there was you.

<u>I need to quiet again.</u>
In the beginning he was not there, so where were they with love, without love? They were all forgotten stars, and it was okay. The universe had got her. In the beginning, they already knew the ending but still they were afraid. Even in the beginning, she loved him and she told him this but he was not there and she had never met him and maybe hardly knew him so her words were for no one and didn't matter but regardless, she said it.

Some say this was an act of most terrible creation but how can she regret what she could not have prevented, something that resounds in the word "regardless", something that dulls eternity in its failure to accept erasure. And she wanted to relate this to the moon again but it didn't work so it was one more thing about words. And once again, she was sorry for her existence but she could not in that moment prevent it, for she would try to give everything of herself.

<u>beyond the gates</u>
in the garden of heaven the creatures walk with hands linked in the
language of the sky.
no i cannot characterize it so i cut my hair
i fall for nobody and quickly,
so quickly
a rain maybe to embrace the sullen earth
drench us in the tears of a melancholy god who just sobbed
nothing all over me and over you too.
please don's be so afraid even
as the sunlight turns me over
even as to release the windowpane
in rain's sweet sufferings.
i don't forget easy anything of
the light earth
nor the colossal sky
for the body aches of universe.
we wandered into a great unknown
the sky was in an impassive storm
and the streetlights lit the way
we could not move or feel anything.
the abrasions of ourselves
against the midnight dark of a new terrible unreality.

the moon spoke little words to her and she pebbled them. openly she
waited
a wound of all that was existence her. he was seeking
an undoing. the sun rose every day and no one said anything of it.
she was. there was a haunting landscape of sound.
the blind came in masses to embrace one another and cry into the
spaces they could not see.
there was no true inhibition but you and i standing there and across the
path
a crow enjoyed a squirrel corpse, only pausing for passing cars.
the migrant workers walked a line and the sun hit them first. he
wanted to leave something behind
but everything came alive only through absence. it was the terrible
womb of the world.
her creation was a shadow to her apology but nothing took her away.

before, we were looking outward
into the aftermath of everything there is a shrouding light and this is
where nobody goes
easy the slopes into a region of sky that cannot be described if seen
such a terrible joy that we clutched our own
faces and could breathe a whole entire nothingness back into our
frail cosmic bones. i came upon the earth one day
and it was surrender.

<u>the sadness of the snow:</u>
though the sky is all heavy but after the snowflakes flutter in unreality
it gets dim and otherworldly and suddenly it's just you and your
interminable breath and it's oddly comforting, the universe snug
against your chin;

is in how it falls
and how it falls

ABOUT THE AUTHOR

Elena grew up in the DC area, lived briefly in Berlin, Johannesburg, and NYC and currently studies at Bard College. She's been published in over a hundred literary magazines over the past few years. She is the winner of four poetry contests, including Word Works Young Poets'. Her poetry has been exhibited at the Greater Reston Art Center and at Arterie Fine Art Gallery. Check out her past poetry books, "we'll beachcomb for their broken bones" (Red Ochre Press, 2014), "a little luminescence" (Allbook-Books, 2011) and "the reason for rain" (Coffeetown Press, 2015). Her visual art has won her several awards. Go to o-mourning-dove.tumblr.com to see her latest artwork.

www.ingramcontent.com/pod-product-compliance
Lightning Source LLC
Chambersburg PA
CBHW071428040426
42445CB00012BA/1299